Jolly Hungry Jack

Written by Carrie Weston

Illustrated by Nick Schon

Jack was jolly hungry.

Dad was cooking the dinner.

"How many potatoes do you want for your dinner?" he called from the kitchen.

Jack just thought. He thought
jolly hungry thoughts.

Maybe one potato, thought Jack.
Then chips and chocolate ice-cream.

Or two potatoes,
with three fishfingers, tomato ketchup
and baked beans.

Jack's belly began to rumble.

He thought some more.
How about four big baked potatoes,
followed by five sizzling sausages
with spaghetti, crisps and a cola?

Then, maybe, six red apples,
seven ripe bananas
and yellow custard.

After that he would eat
eight **king-size** chocolate bars
and a bit of cheese.

Jack could smell dinner
cooking in the kitchen.

No, maybe he would have
nine burgers with ten burger buns.
The last bun he would dip in
a big mug of cocoa.

After that, maybe lots of lovely lime jelly...

Suddenly Dad called
from the kitchen.
"JACK! How many potatoes
do you want for your dinner?"

Jack felt jolly sick.

"Just one potato, please,"
he said quietly.